A PIECE
OF HEAVEN
ON EARTH

By:

To: Scott & Marisa,
May God Bless you now &
forever! Love, Aunt Cindy

Cynthia Yates Soles

John, 3:16

AuthorHouse™
1663 Liberty Drive
Bloomington, IN 47403
www.authorhouse.com
Phone: 1-800-839-8640

First published by AuthorHouse 10/23/2009

ISBN: 978-1-4490-3692-8 (sc)
ISBN: 978-1-4490-3693-5 (hc)
IBN: 978-1-4490-3755-0 (e)

Library of Congress Control Number: 2009911173

All Scripture quotations are taken from the Holy Bible: The New International Version, copyright 1977 by the International Bible Society.

Printed in the United States of America
Bloomington, Indiana

This book is printed on acid-free paper.

WITH GOD ALL THINGS ARE POSSIBLE!

I am thankful to God for all of the wonderful people he has put in my journey of life. And I know it is only through His guidance, mercy, love and grace that this book became a reality. I give God all of the honor and glory in everything that I have accomplished.

THIS BOOK IS
IN LOVING MEMORY:
OF

EMMA RUSSO YATES

She encouraged me to write and
"NEVER GIVE UP ON MY DREAMS!"

She believed in me when I didn't believe in myself, and words can't express how much her support, encouragement and love meant to me. Her faith and unconditional love made a great impact on my life. The way she lived set the example of a strong role model, which made a lasting impression on me to become a better mother and person. Her sweet spirit inspired many and lives on in eternity.

DEDICATIONS:

To my daughters: Sarah Soles Dongilli and Marlena Soles.

Your love has enlightened my heart, and I am blessed to have such wonderful daughters. It is an honor and privilege to be a part of your lives. I am grateful to God for the times we share, and the pleasure as I watch you grow each new day.

And this book is also dedicated to my grandsons, Domenick and Trustin Dongilli.

My favorite saying, as a small child, lives on in my grandsons: I love you bushels and bushels up to the sky! Your smiles and laughter fill my heart with unbelievable joy. No matter what might be going on around me, your presence brightens my day. I love you with all of my heart, and thank God for you every day. Your Nana Banana will always love you!

CONTENTS

FOREWORD

When Cynthia first asked me to write a foreword for her book, my first reaction was, "Why me?" After all, most forewords I have ever read were written by authors themselves, and for a Christian book, we would expect at least a pastor, right? I am neither. What I am is someone who has known Cynthia for more than thirty years as friends, as family (our husbands were cousins,) and as Christian sisters. We have raised our children together, vacationed together, prayed together, led worship services together, and planned women's retreats together. And all the while, I watched Cynthia live through much of what she shares in this book. I saw her struggling, but always praying too. Afflicted, but also blessed.

Her life and her story have encouraged and inspired me, and I know they will do the same for all who read these pages. Cynthia calls her book the story of extraordinary blessings experienced by an "ordinary" person. Now that I think about it, I may be the right person for this job after all!

Thanks, Cynthia, for sharing your adventure with me!

Love,
Barb

Foreword written by Barbara Vandermer

INTRODUCTION

My story is about an ordinary person, with an ordinary life, ME! As I share the miracles of my life, hopefully you will be inspired. My mother passed away on May 3, 2009, after a long battle with cancer. She had been the inspiration in my life; even as she suffered, she still put the needs of her family and friends before her own. No matter how hard the situation became, she never wanted to give up! Faith and hope embraced her life as she kept moving forward. Eventually, the time came and we knew the doctors did everything possible; however, nothing would make her well. How helpless I felt as I watched my mother's body shut down from this horrible disease. I know first hand how hard it is to watch a loved one suffer. At one time or another, all of us will have some kind of pain or suffering to endure. During these difficulties in our lives, how we cope emotionally, physically, and spiritually will determine if we will move forward to overcome these obstacles or give up on life. I truly believe as we endure these hardships, we can grow stronger and still achieve the joy and peace of God in all things.

Throughout her life, mom really enjoyed putting together jigsaw puzzles. After her cancer surgery, and being so limited in the things that she could do, she spent a lot of her energy on her favorite past time. I watched her build the puzzles, day after day, without looking at the picture on the box. I was fascinated how the puzzles came together so easily for Mom. Life reminds me of a giant jigsaw puzzle; until all the pieces fit together, you cannot appreciate the whole picture. Since Mom once fit so perfectly in my life, when that piece was missing I felt so alone, afraid, empty and lost. Slowly but surely, as I picked the pieces up, one at a time, my life went on.

Mom was definitely a big part of my life, and since

she was the one that encouraged me to write, I decided to follow my dream, and put bits and pieces of my life in a book. In the pages ahead, I share some of the many experiences of hardships, heartache, miracles, peace, and God's love, to encourage others, not to give up! Hopefully, as you read, *A Piece of Heaven on Earth*, you will be inspired, as you embrace the pieces in your own life, to believe what God has done for me, an ordinary person, He will do for you. My prayer is that you would know God as your Heavenly Father, and you too will experience a piece of heaven on earth.

Chapter one

GOD'S HAND OF PROTECTION

I was born on a Sunday in the year 1956, the sixteenth day of September, the daughter of Emma and Nelson Yates. I have five siblings and we grew up in Monessen, a small mill town, on the outskirts of Pittsburgh, Pennsylvania. Being the daughter of a mill worker, my childhood was as normal as could be. When I watch the old movies of my life, it brings back the precious memories of my past. I had to squint when looking at the camera with that big bright light that shone in my face. Even without any audio on our old tapes, I can still hear those familiar sounds. The images showed how hard my mother and father worked to build our house. I did not realize how much my parents sacrificed for us. It had to be

1

overwhelming with six children living in one household, in a small foundation, as they worked long hard hours to build our home. Since I could not see the whole picture, I did not think my parents would ever accomplish their dream. However, I marveled at what they did achieve, and learned a valuable lesson: life is hard work, but if you don't give up, you will succeed.

My parents also found the time to tend to our needs and be a part of our fun. The sound of our laughter is what you heard, as we ran around the yard, slid down the hillside in a cardboard box, or hit a balloon in the air. I enjoyed jumping rope, hopscotch, and doing cartwheels from one end of the yard to the other. Mom taught me how to play jacks, and when I won first place in a local contest, she clipped my name out of the newspaper and put my little trophy and ribbon on top of the television. We definitely enjoyed the simple things in life. Those special moments hidden deep within my heart will always be treasured.

Living with four brothers and a sister, I often went off alone to have some quiet time. I would take our collie for long walks, in a large field next to our home. I had a peaceful spot underneath a tree where I prayed. At a young age, I did not realize the importance of being alone and praying, underneath that tree. We were raised with basic beliefs about God, but it wouldn't be until later, I would recognize what an important piece God would become to me.

Looking over my past, and remembering a big highlight in my life, I would be one out of many to get the chance to experience the excitement when Monessen became a part of history. Time went by so quickly, it seems like a hundred years ago, that President John F. Kennedy visited our little town. People were elbow-to-elbow, and it looked like a sea of faces on the streets. Mom had a tight grip on my hand so I would not be lost in the massive crowd. I was amazed to watch as so many gathered together to see the President and hear his speech. As a small child, the joy and excitement I had experienced would become one out of many that I will never forget.

When the mill downsized, a lot of people were affected, and had to leave town to find work, but we stayed, because my father worked long enough to take an early retirement. One good thing came out of this difficulty: Dad had more time to spend with us. He enjoyed fishing and taking us along. On one occasion, while my little brother picked cattails along the side of the lake, he accidently fell into the water. He had already been floating face down when my father jumped in and pulled him to safety. He was white as a sheet, his lips were blue, and his little body was motionless. I still remember the terror on Mom's face as she watched everything take place. Everyone was really upset until they realized that he would be alright. This incident could have ended differently, if not for Dad's quick actions and God's hand of protection on my brother's life.

Psalm 4:8 (I will lie down and sleep in peace, for you alone, O Lord, make me dwell in safety.) (NIV)

We were always surrounded by family and friends. If they were not gathered at our home, we would travel to visit them. All of us would pile into our white station wagon. Before the doors were even closed, Dad had already told us, "Don't lean on the car door!" One afternoon, as we traveled to my grandmother's house, I leaned on the car door. Suddenly, Dad was startled by the sound of a constant honking horn. A man driving behind us saw my car door swinging back and forth, and desperately tried to warn my father. As dad glanced in his side mirror, he saw that my door had opened. Quickly he slammed on his brakes and I fell out of the car. Incredibly, the tire stopped inches away from my head. Some how shaking so badly, Dad managed to pick me up off of the ground. That day still haunts my father! Since, I was so young, I really did not see that piece of my life as such a big deal. It wouldn't be until years later when I saw the whole picture, that I appreciated God's hand of protection that had been with me that day.

Psalm 5:11 (But let all who take refuge in you be glad; let them ever sing of joy. Spread your protection over them that those who love your name may rejoice in you.) (NIV)

Over the years, we all did our part to help lighten the work load for our parents. Ironing was one chore that I enjoyed the most; it was definitely my favorite. Because my mom worried I would get burned, it took a lot of coaxing before she would give in. Mom ironed the big pieces of clothing, and then I would be allowed to press the wrinkles out of the hankies, doilies, and pillow cases. One morning, after mom finished ironing some dresses, she left the room to hang them up, and within seconds she heard my cries. I wanted to surprise her by ironing the next article of clothing on top of the laundry basket. Mom knew when she heard me yell what had happened. When I bumped into the ironing board, I knocked over the iron which burned the imprint of the tip and holes into my arm. I had some of the biggest and ugliest blisters our doctor said that he had ever seen. I was so glad that the bandages kept my arm covered for a long period of time. It took months of treatments before we saw any improvements on my second and third degree burns. Back in those days, doctors made house calls, and our family doctor made plenty of trips back and forth to keep on top of my care. Life is so different today; without the proper insurance you are lucky if a doctor will even examine you. We were told, "I would need surgery because it would be impossible for my scars to ever go away." But with God all things are possible and my scars disappeared!

Matthew 19:26 (Jesus looked at them and said, "With man this is impossible, but with God all things are possible.") (NIV)

On a cold and frosty day, when I was in seventh grade, Dad drove my sister and me to school. As we approached the front of the building, I saw my classmates were standing outside waiting for the bell to ring. My father pulled up to the curb. As I gathered my books from the back seat, I shut the door and Dad drove away. Unfortunately, my coat was caught in the car door. I tried desperately to get my father's attention, so I ran along the side of the car and pounded on the window pane. When that did not work I had to yell for him to stop! The shrill sound of my voice made him turn to see what had happened. When he saw me run frantically down the side of the road, he immediately stopped. As I opened the door to release my coat I heard a huge roar of laughter. My classmates thought it was funny and I was the joke. Being a teenager, I was embarrassed instead of thinking how badly I could have been hurt. Looking back on that day, surely it was not funny, but giggling as I write this, I could

picture that piece of my life as one hilarious scene.

Psalm 63:7-8 (Because you are my help, I sing in the shadow of your wings, my soul clings to you: your right hand upholds me.) (NIV)

My father had quarter horses and I loved to ride. I

took Western and English riding lessons, but I would have

to say, my favorite way to ride, was bareback. At eighteen

years old, I went on vacation with my sister and her family,

and we stayed on a farm. On our trip an opportunity arose

for me to ride, and with my love for horses, how could I

possibly refuse, especially, on a beautiful sunny day, upon

a gorgeous black stallion, in one of the largest corn fields I

had ever seen? We galloped between rows and rows of

huge corn stalks. The country air sure smelled a lot nicer

than the thick gray smog from the smoke stacks in the middle of downtown Monessen. How quiet and peaceful! The only sounds were the horses' hooves and the sweet chirping of the birds. We were all having a great time, but strangely, the longer that we rode, my side began to hurt. The pain was unbearable, and I barely made it back to the barn to dismount. Finally, my pain eased up and I was thankful, because I knew we had to travel home in the morning.

During the night I had a dull pain, but it was nothing compared to the discomfort when I was riding. The next day it took us about six hours before we arrived home. We were only home for about thirty minutes when the pain became unbearable again. My brother-in-law and mother rushed me to the hospital, and within minutes they were wheeling me to the operating room. My appendix burst and the poison went through my body. After my operation, the doctor told my mother, "If I would not have had medical attention when I did, I would not be here today." Once again, it was not my time, and thankfully God's mighty hand was upon me!

Psalm 41:3 (The Lord will sustain him on his sickbed and restore him from his bed of illness.) (NIV)

Mom prayed while I was in surgery, but that was not a surprise to me, because praying was a big piece of her everyday life. Prayers from a mother's heart are sincere and special. She had taught me God, family, and friends, were very important in life. Her example of love she set, and valuable wisdom that she had handed down would have a great impact on my life. But I would not understand how much, until I was old enough to know the importance of God. Looking over my childhood, and remembering my

past, we were not rich but we had what money could not

buy---love for God and one another.

John 13:34 ("A new command I give you: Love one another, As I have loved you, so you must love one another.") (NIV)

Dear Reader,

Looking over your childhood, are there pieces that you see differently and now can appreciate God's hand in your life?

Do you remember the people that have impacted your life in who you have become today?

Do you enjoy the simple things in life?

Remember: Everyone needs quiet time to be alone and

pray.

*Emma Yates
(Cynthia's Mother)*

*Nelson Yates
(Cynthia's Father)*

*On Right: Cynthia
with her parents
Nelson and Emma*

*Below: Cynthia as a
baby*

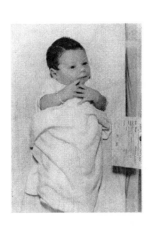

Top photo: Cynthia with her Godparents/Aunt Martha & Uncle Paul DiBattista

Bottom photo: Cynthia with her Aunt Martha

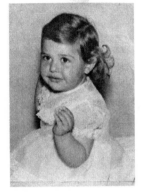

Top Left: brother
Wayne
Top Right brothers
Mark & John

Center Right Cynthia

Bottom Left
Sister Freda and
brother Nelson Jr.

*Top Right Cynthia
with her grandmother
Sarah Yates*

*Center Right Cynthia
with her Uncle John
Yates
Bottom Cynthia with
her Uncle James Yates*

Top Left:
Cynthia on Big Red

Bottom Right
Nelson Yates on Poco
Chambee

Chapter 2

MY DAUGHTERS' MIRACLES

After graduation, my friends talked about which college they would be attending or how many job interviews they had, but I did not have any ambition to further my education or to work. The desire of my heart was to get married and have children. At the age of twenty-one, I married a man who had a daughter and a son, so I became a wife and mother over night. The weekends we shared together as a family were so enjoyable because his children brought joy and fun to our home. However, I still wanted to have a child of my own. It devastated me that doctor after doctor told me I would never have a child. In spite of all the test results, I strongly believed I would have a child. I told my family and friends that I would have a daughter and she would be born on January fourth. Yes, a lot of people thought that I had gone off of the deep end. No wonder, I told them I would have a little girl and even the day that she would be born.

There are so many miracles in the Bible, but one of my favorite, is when Sarah, a ninety- year-old woman gave birth. We would be truly blessed just to live that long; I could not even imagine giving birth and raising a child at ninety. Well, at age twenty-four, I experienced a wonderful miracle, the birth of my first daughter. God had blessed me with my very own Sarah born on January fourth!

Genesis 17:17 (Abraham at one hundred years old and Sarah at ninety years old would bear a child.) (NIV)

Twenty months later we had our second child, Marlena. At age twenty-five, I thought having two precious daughters, would be an exciting adventure for me. However, it became an unbelievable journey with many responsibilities. At six weeks old, Marlena had to be hospitalized and what a challenge she became to her doctor. He had no idea why her lips would turn blue, so she was immediately transferred, by ambulance, to Children's Hospital in Pittsburgh. While Marlena was strapped to the gurney she started to cry, so the nurse held her in her arms to comfort her. Unexpectedly, when a car pulled out in front of us, the ambulance driver swerved quickly to avoid being hit. Helplessly, I watched as the nurse hit her head. Although she tried her best to hold onto my daughter, she fell from her arms and rolled. Within seconds the blood from the nurse's head covered my little darling dressed in pink satin and bows. Thankfully, Marlena and I were both okay. Unfortunately, the nurse had to have stitches that day.

Psalm 16:1 (Keep me safe, O God, for in you I take refuge.) (NIV)

After an endoscopy, bronchoscopy, electrocardiogram, and pulmonary function tests, Marlena was diagnosed with severe laryngomalacia. She was considered a stridor baby. Her larynx was soft and would collapse inward when she inhaled, which caused her to experience some difficulty breathing. When she would take a breath, it made a high pitch noise. My mother said that she sounded like a pressure cooker. And while she slept, her breathing became so shallow that many times she would stop breathing for a few seconds. Before Marlena would be discharged, we had to learn CPR on an infant. I had been certified once before so I knew the proper procedures, but I needed to repeat the class so I could update the requirements of recertification. We were not able to leave her with any one unless they knew CPR, but nobody wanted the responsibility to watch her anyway. I really understood because I knew how afraid I was every second of the day.

I also had to learn how to operate an apnea monitor. She wore a belt with sensory wires around her chest, and then I had to hook the wires into a monitoring unit with an alarm. We had to tell the electric company that she was on a monitor so that they could alert us just in case the electricity went out. How many times the same fears went through my mind, "What if she stops breathing and I can't resuscitate her?" And I will never forget all of the awful nightmares. I would dream night after night she stopped breathing, and no matter how hard I tried, there wasn't anything I could do. They seemed so real that I would be awakened with fear and tears that streamed down my cheeks. I slept in my clothes plenty of nights to be prepared for the worst.

One evening during a bad storm, the alarm went off. The electric company called immediately to inform us that they were dealing with the problem and it would be repaired as soon as possible. Believe me, we already knew, before the phone rang, because when that alarm went off it made such a loud noise, I thought the whole neighborhood could hear. I read the Bible by flashlight in the rocking chair next to her crib. I was so relieved when the storm ended and the lights went back on.

I remember on August 29, 1982, the day of her baptism, you could hardly hear the minister's voice over the strange noise that she made. The first eight months of her life were so stressful that I do not remember a day that went by that I had any peaceful rest. Definitely, at that time in my life, I thought that nothing could be any worse. Even in those restless days and nights, God gave me strength and His grace was with me, because I never had to administer CPR on Marlena.

Isaiah 40:29-31 (He gives strength to the weary, and increases the power of the weak. Even youths grow tired and weary, and young men stumble and fall; but those who hope in the Lord will renew their strength. They will soar on wings of eagles; they will run and not grow weary, they will walk and not be faint.) (NIV)

Doctors told us Marlena would never walk. Marlena had fourteen casts for bone corrections because of deformities in her feet. On Sunday evenings, I had to soak her feet until the old casts would fall off. Then on Monday mornings we would travel to Pittsburgh for the serial casts to be reapplied. We went through this procedure for several weeks. I will always remember on Thanksgiving Day, Marlena's feet were in casts, and Sarah fell down three steps and hurt her left arm. There I stood holding Marlena while Sarah had a cast put on her little arm. On Christmas Day, the conversation would not be about their cute little red velvet dresses with white eyelet lace; instead everyone talked about their tiny casts.

I was so happy when she no longer had to wear the serial casts. The next step for Marlena was wearing special shoes, and they were the most hideous little white shoes I had ever seen. They laced up the front, and you could watch as she wiggled her little toes, because the tips of the shoes were cut out. And the soles were turned in the opposite direction than on a regular shoe. How funny they looked! Everybody thought that I had put her shoes on the wrong feet. It did not matter; everywhere that we went somebody would comment that I had her shoes on wrong. I often wondered if people thought that I cut the tips out of her shoes. How could anyone not see that these were not normal shoes! At first, I would go into this long explanation; when I got tired of explaining to people, I politely thanked them and walked away.

After months of doctor appointments, x-rays, casts, and special shoes had ended, Marlena fell and broke her ankle. However, this cast was different; Marlena cried and hit her foot against anything she could, because it was hurting her and she wanted it off. I knew something had to be wrong and I insisted that it be removed. Here was a child that had more casts at her age than some adults have in a life time. Once the cast had been removed they discovered she had a sore, very deep and infected in the heel of her foot, which could have caused blood poisoning.

The healing process went slowly, because of many months of treatments, and this delayed her walking ability even more. I was thankful she had the proper care in time and did not get blood poisoning. Marlena did beat the odds after she went through such a long ordeal. Not only did she walk, she took ballet and tap dance classes. I praised God for his help daily, but most of all, Marlena's miracle to walk!

Psalm 9:1 (I will praise you, O Lord, with all my heart; I will tell of all your wonders.) (NIV)

We had a few years, without any broken bones, until Sarah fell off monkey bars in the park and broke her right arm. Then the following year while she rode her bicycle with her friend, she fell and broke her left arm again. This time her bone penetrated though the skin, and we were thankful that her friend did get her home quickly, because she needed proper medical attention fast. As soon as the nurse saw her arm, they tended to her promptly; they found a qualified surgeon to operate. We continued with her care with months of treatments. After Marlena's fifteen casts, and Sarah's three broken arms, no wonder Sarah often talked about becoming a nurse. At that time we had no idea how the people and the procedures were impacting Sarah's life. Today she has devoted her life to helping others as an x-ray technician.

1 John 5: 14-15 (This is the confidence we have in approaching God: that if we ask anything according to his will, he hears us. And if we know he hears us—whatever we ask—we know that we have what we asked of him.) (NIV)

There were so many different doctors in Marlena's life, and the word NEVER was used frequently by most of them. Now we were told that Marlena would never talk. At age three, she should have been expressing herself with language; instead she pointed to things. The doctors blamed her many ear infections for her lack of speech. Not only that, she had to take a lot of antibiotics which made her little body immune to them, so the infections damaged her ears. Since the prescribed medications no longer worked, other measures had to be taken. She had to have bilateral myringotomy surgery to place tympanostomy tubes inside of her ears. This would help the air flow in and out of her middle ear to stop the repeated ear infections. When the tubes slipped out of place, it caused many other problems, and she had countless surgeries to replace them.

One afternoon, as she watched television, I noticed that she had put her ear on the screen. Immediately, I knew that something was wrong. Over the years, from all of the infections and the tubes; she had holes in both of her ears which caused her to be completely deaf. The doctor said, he could fix the holes, but the scar tissue was so bad, he could not do anything that would help her to hear. We were sent to a school where they taught sign language, and I bought books to teach myself.

Marlena had been scheduled for an operation to repair the holes, and on our way to the hospital, she said, that God had healed her during the night. Amazingly, when the doctor examined Marlena, he was shocked to find that the holes were gone. Then he performed a hearing test and she was perfectly fine. Her testimony touched my heart, as well as others, and the doctor could not believe what he saw. The holes were healed and now she could hear! We were in amazement by the awesome power of God!

Mark 5:34 (Daughter, your faith has healed you. Go in peace and be freed from your suffering.) (NIV)

Marlena had allergies, bronchitis, and asthma, which made her sick all of the time. Both of my daughters had so many upper respiratory infections, that they had to have their tonsils removed. So I decided to have them admitted to the hospital for their tonsillectomies on the same day. The nurses could not believe any mother would have their children's tonsils removed on the same day. Jokingly, they said I had to be very brave or very crazy! At that time, I did not know what they meant, but I did agree afterward that I made a huge mistake.

Sarah had her tonsils removed first. Then Marlena underwent an adenotonsillectomy, an operation to remove her adenoids and tonsils. After they were discharged, Sarah became dehydrated and looked like a rag doll in my arms. Immediately, she was readmitted for three more days, until she was well enough to be released into my care. I was so happy not to be running back and forth between the hospital and home. However, Sarah was only home for one night, when Marlena started to bleed and was rushed to the hospital. Even after she stopped bleeding, they had to keep Marlena for observation. Finally, she was discharged and what a relief to be back home.

We were back on track for about three weeks when I became very ill. Since I had been so busy taking care of the girls, I did not take care of myself. I had my share of upper respiratory infections too. The time came and I had to have my tonsils removed, but at my age it would be a lot harder on me. So many people told me their horror stories, and I already knew what the girls went through, but everybody's experiences are different. This was a difficult time with a lot of pain and suffering that we all went through, but I knew that all of these burdens would eventually end.

Matthew 11:28 ("Come to me, all you who are weary and burdened, and I will give you rest.") (NIV)

We surely had our share of trials and tribulations in the past years, but I hung onto the fact that in time they would all be resolved. Until one day, Marlena was diagnosed with osteochondritis, a disease which affects the joints. It was hard for me to believe her diagnosis, since this disease was found in older children, teenagers and adults. Her tests also showed that her bones were growing too fast for her age. Her specialists decided she would need Lupron shots, which were not FDA approved on such a young child. After consulting with many different specialists, we finally made the decision and went ahead with the shots. Not only would they slow down her maturing process, there could be possible side effects. This extreme measure of treatment was very scary, plus we had to pay all of the expenses, because her insurance company would not take any responsibility if something went wrong.

They kept a close eye on her, administering many blood tests and MRIs to keep us updated on her progress. After one MRI, we would not be prepared for what came next. After studying the images, what a big disappointment for us to learn, she had a brain tumor, and absolutely no operation could be performed. With this new information, it all made sense. We now knew why she had so many difficulties and delayed developments.

Each time that an MRI was performed, the tumor grew larger, and she started to have mini seizures. Of course, there would be more consultations, specialists, medications and medical treatments added to our lives. All I did was go from one doctor's appointment to the next, and back and forth to hospitals, for test after test. Finally, when I felt I came to the end of my rope, there would be a new outcome: no longer could the tumor be found and her seizures stopped! I was grateful to God for answering our prayers!

---

1 Thessalonians 5:16-18 ("to be joyful always; pray continually; give thanks in all circumstances, for this is God's will for you in Christ Jesus.") (NIV)

Dear Reader,

Do you remember past trials and tribulations?

Are you going through a difficult time and feel that you are

at the end of your rope?

Remember: Pray continually; give thanks in all

circumstances and believe God answers

prayers! God does Miracles!

Chapter 3

PUZZLED PIECES

Marlena's life was full of circumstances that could not be changed. For instance, she had to attend special classes and will always need some kind of care. She'll never use a stove, drive a car, get married, have children, or even be left alone. She will not experience life as an adult; she will stay a child in a woman's body. Even with the tumor gone, her body would mature, but her mind would stay the same.

Trying to make sense out of these puzzling pieces in her life, I became angry and fearful. Frankly, I had so much fear and anger built up inside, my heart grew hard and bitter, and a part of me had died. I was emotionally numb; it took everything out of me to keep up with my daily routine. I existed from day to day; I went through the motions instead of living. My life was so terrible that I could not wait until evening came to climb back into bed so I could forget my problems. The heartache I felt was awful! Being a mother and not being able to do anything to make my daughter's life any easier was very disturbing to me.

Psalm 42:5 (My soul is downcast, O my soul? Why so disturbed within me? Put your hope in God, for I will yet praise him, my Savior and my God.) (NIV)

Quickly, the outrageous medical bills stacked high in my mail. With these extra pieces of stress and anxiety added to my life, soon my health began to fail. Over many years, I battled with weight loss, flu like symptoms, pain, and fatigue. I was sent to many specialists that studied my

44

case. Since they could not diagnose me, I was prescribed different kinds of medications, mainly for depression, so I seriously wondered was I lazy or just crazy! If this entire situation weren't bad enough, I could not tolerate any of the medications which made my symptoms worse.

Finally, after years of tests, they discovered I had Epstein Barr virus, chronic fatigue syndrome, and fibromyalgia. I was neither lazy nor crazy! Today, these illnesses are common in the medical field and viewed very differently. I felt that I had overcome a big obstacle in my life; at last we could put names to my symptoms, but no relief for the pain. Since the pain did not subside, I had to have a biopsy on my kidney. I became overwhelmed when diagnosed with IgM nephropathy; my own immune system is attacking my kidney. At this point in my life, being so exhausted and with all of the pain, I had lost hope! Even after the big break through and all the miracles I had already been blessed with, I still felt helpless and hopeless deep down inside.

Being distraught over my health issues, Marlena's problems, and my husband's work demands, I became frustrated. I felt so alone and eventually our marriage ended. Becoming a single parent, I felt like pieces of my life were thrown everywhere and nothing seemed to fit, I became confused and disconnected. Did you ever try to build a jigsaw puzzle and you couldn't find the right piece? The frustration builds until you just give up and walk away. Well, that's how I felt about my puzzled life.

Years later Marlena became ill again, and after her diagnosis the doctors told us, she would never live a long life. She was diagnosed with mitochondrial disease by two specialists in Pittsburgh. They explained mitochondria are responsible to produce ninety percent of the energy for our body to sustain life. And they told me some of the problems of this disease such as developmental delays, mental retardation, respiratory complications, seizures, and deafness, all of which Marlena had experienced. After going to so many specialists, over many years, we never knew why she had so many difficulties in her life. When they were done explaining to me what would happen to her, they came right out and said, "We are sorry to say, but your daughter is going to die." They kept asking me if I understood; I guess I was in shock, because I did not say anything. The doctors were ninety-nine percent sure she had this dreaded illness.

Fearing I had little time left with my daughter, so I decided to take Marlena to Disney World. We stayed in Florida for two weeks and had a great time. When we returned home, I had a message on my answering machine, to call the doctor. I waited until the next morning, because no news could have been any worse than what I had already received. When I called, I was informed, Marlena did not have the horrible disease, that they had made a mistake. Unbelievable as it seemed, I did not believe they made such an awful mistake, I believed it was another great miracle in our lives.

Psalm 34:4 (I sought the Lord, and he answered me; he delivered me from all of my fears.) (NIV)

Well, these were the pieces that I had to deal with in my life. Having so many difficulties to endure had overwhelmed me. I often asked myself, "Where is God in all this mess?" I had sickness, divorce, financial problems, pain, and somewhere along my journey I blamed God for all of the bad in my life. I was extremely exhausted and knew I could not carry this heavy load alone any longer.

And suddenly, I realized before life got the best of me, I had to make a choice fast, and the only option that I had was to trust God, instead of blaming him. I had to stop complaining and accept the things that I could not change. Sure I prayed, I went to God, but mainly when things were bad. When I stopped focusing on my problems, and committed to studying God's word daily and praying with a prayer partner, I could see the whole picture.

As I struggled through those years, now it is clear for me to see, everything that I needed was right in front of me. It is not a coincidence that the family and friends in our lives are there for a reason. My family and friends helped me clean, take care of my car, did my yard work, drove me to appointments, and supported me financially. I don't know where I would have been today without so many wonderful and caring people in my life. God gave me what I needed in His time, and His timing is always right. God was in everyone and everything!

Psalm 107:41 (But He lifted the needy out of their affliction and increased their families like flocks.) (NIV)

My Bible study and prayer eventually lead me to find the enormous piece to my life which had been missing, the Holy Spirit. The Bible teaches us in John 14:20 (On that day you will realize that I am in my Father, and you are in me, and I am in you.) (NIV) I believe in God, and I believe that Jesus is God's son, but I guess it was hard to comprehend the Spirit of God living in me. In John 3, Jesus teaches Nicodemus, ("I tell you the truth, no one can see the kingdom of God unless he is born again.") (NIV) Nicodemus did not understand and asked, (Surely he cannot enter a second time into his mother's womb to be born!") (NIV) Nicodemus did not understand and neither did I. But Jesus was offering a rebirth, a new beginning, a new life to Nicodemus, and that was what I needed and wanted for my life. Finally, even with all of the puzzling pieces going on in my life, I began enjoying living again.

Psalm 13: 5-6 ("But I will trust in your unfailing love, my heart rejoices in your salvation. I will sing to the Lord, for he has been good to me.) (NIV)

Dear Reader,

Are you facing financial difficulty?

Are there some puzzling pieces in your life making you frustrated?

Are you angry about something or somebody and just want to walk away?

Remember: God is good and trust in His unfailing love!

Chapter 4

NEW OUTLOOK ON LIFE

My new outlook on life is what I needed for what came next. My father had a heart attack and had open heart surgery. All of us were at his bedside, as he talked to his mother on the phone, to let her know his progress. My father visited his mother every day, so he could not wait to be discharged to see her. Little did he know, it would be only three days after he came home, that my grandmother would have a massive heart attack and pass away. How quickly lives are changed forever! We are here today and within that split second we can be gone!

The third person to experience a heart attack would be Mom. Reliving Dad's heart attack we knew what to expect in the coming days. It was unbelievable how many people were scheduled for open heart surgeries. Looking around the hospital waiting room, I saw so many frightened loved ones, waiting for some kind of news. I did spend a lot of time at the hospital while mom was recuperating. It amazed me to see how quickly they wanted their patients up and on their feet and out the door, but Mom contracted a staph infection so her recovery went slowly. She had home care for quite some time, and I slept at her bedside, as much as possible, so I would be close by if she needed anything.

While I took care of Mom, I had spent a lot of time away from home; this made a perfect opportunity for somebody to break into our house, and one night someone did. I was thankful that we were not there, but I knew eventually we would have to return home. Certainly I was apprehensive, but I tried to alleviate my fears. Surely whoever broke in would not do it again, and especially while we were there. Unfortunately, the first night we were home, I had to call 911! The police found a crowbar on the ground which they believed was used to pry the back door open.

My main concern of course was the safety of my daughters. We found another home, and moved as fast as possible. Not long afterwards, I was watching the evening news, and was shocked to see our old neighborhood on the television screen. The police were arresting a man who beat up a few of the neighbors and then murdered the elderly woman who lived next door to us. It was comforting to know, without a doubt, God had protected and guided us far away from that situation.

Psalm 23:4 (Even though I walk through the valley of the shadow of death, I will fear no evil, for you are with me; your rod and your staff, they comfort me.) (NIV)

Life continued to have its ups and downs. It would not be long before my uncle would need my family's help. He was diagnosed with stomach cancer. He never married so he did not have any children of his own. When he became ill, his only wish was to die at home. My father and his younger brother both agreed to take care of him. He was sent home on hospice and I knew they would also need my help. My uncle was always there for everyone, and now it was our turn to care for him. I remember how he was a comfort to his sister-in-law as he sat at her bedside, until cancer took her life. And I did not forget how he helped out with Mom and Dad as they went through their operations. Despite his own diagnosis of cancer, he put the needs of others before himself. When his neighbor became ill, he helped by transporting him to and from the hospital for his treatments. When his neighbor died, he watered the flowers on his grave. He continued to help others with his wisdom, finances, and guidance for as long as his health permitted.

Family, friends and neighbors showed their gratitude to him by coming to his aid. They cooked, cut his grass, cleaned his home, sent cards of encouragement, and prayed. To see my uncle receive those blessings of love and caring from others was inspiring. During his last months, his faith continued to be an inspiration to me and others; even in his pain and suffering, he never complained. As I watched him take his last breath, I remembered how he loved and cared for everyone.

It would not be long, after we started to put the pieces back together, that my children would experience tremendous heartache. Once again pieces of their lives were torn apart, when their father passed away from cancer. His example of courage, love, and faith, would be with them forever. In such a short time our family had lost so many to death. It would be easy to give into grief and despair, but I learned an important lesson. Life is so short; it is very important that everyone knows where they will go, once the final piece fits into their lives. Do you know where you will go when that final piece is completed?

John 3:16 ("For God so loved the world that he gave his one and only Son, that whoever believes in him shall not perish but have eternal life.) (NIV)

When my first grandson Domenick was born, the joy in my heart was unbelievable, and every moment that I spend with him is so precious to me. Of course my own children are very dear, but when they were young I dwelled on my problems, instead of the enjoyment I experience now. We learn and grow from past mistakes, but we should not dwell on them. We have old memories to enlighten our hearts, but we must look forward to making new ones, so we can continue living life to the fullest.

When my second grandson Trustin was born, his birth would become a huge piece to solving part of my own puzzling lifetime symptoms. As a newborn, his blood was tested because he had jaundice, and he was diagnosed with G-6-PD, a blood disorder carried through my maternal generation. Later, I learned that I also suffered from G-6-PD; it is an inherited condition, where our bodies don't have enough of the enzyme glucose-6-phosphate dehydrogenase to help the red blood cells function correctly. There is a long list of drugs we cannot take with this condition. We will have to watch what we eat and the medications that we take. At a young age, my grandson will have the proper care, and he will live a healthy normal life. I am grateful he will not have to go through what I did. On the other hand, since I took the wrong medications for many years, my health has been damaged. Now the doctors understand why I could not tolerate the medications prescribed to me in the past.

Although this blood disorder answered some questions, about my mysterious symptoms, I was still ill. After having other tests, my list of illnesses grew, but the main concern would be my diagnosis of Lupus. My mind raced with many questions that I wanted answered. First of all, what was Lupus? How did I get Lupus? Was it all the prescription drugs prescribed to me over the years or did I inherit this awful disease?

Lupus is an autoimmune disease and the cause is unknown. Medications might help, but nothing will cure the sickness and other problems could result from having this disease. Since I have tried so many different medicines in the past and cannot tolerate them, there is nothing that can be done. This will be another hurdle for me to overcome, but I will continue to have confidence in God for his mercy and grace in my time of need.

Hebrews 4: 16 (Let us then approach the throne of grace with confidence, so that we may receive mercy and find grace to help us in our time of need.) (NIV)

Dear Reader,

Are you or somebody you love faced with a mysterious illness?

Have you lost your peace and hope?

Remember: God is always with us, but we have to make the choice to go to Him in faith, so that we may receive mercy and find grace in our time of need!

Top left Wedding Day
Cynthia & Jeff Soles
Top Right
Cynthia, Jeff & Sarah
Soles

Center Right: Sarah
Soles

Bottom left
Cynthia and Marlena
Soles

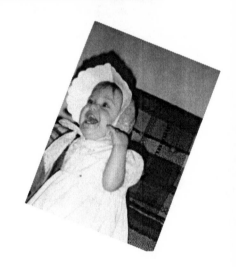

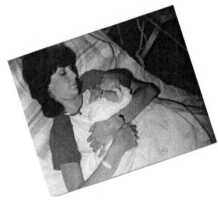

Sarah Soles and her
three casts

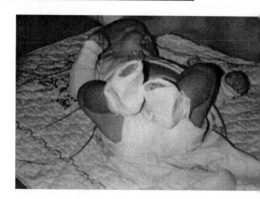

Marlena Soles with casts, her apnea monitor and one of many hospital visits.

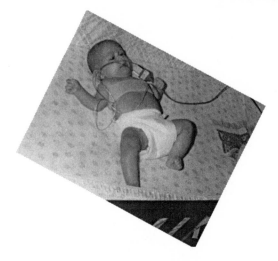

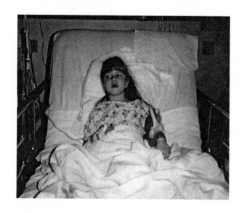

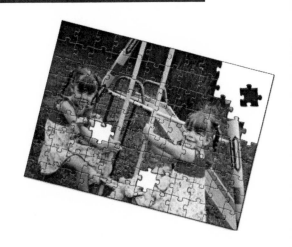

Sarah & Marlena Soles
Cynthia's daughters

*Sarah and Marlena
Soles at the beach*

Sarah & Marlena in
their dancing costumes

*Domenick &
Trustin
Dongilli
Cynthia's
grandsons*

Domenick & Trustin
Dongilli with their
puppy Queenie

73

Top left: Jason
Dongilli and his sons
Domenick & Trustin
after Jason came
back from Iraq

Center right photos
Domenick & Trustin

Bottom left Sarah
Soles Dongilli with
her son Trustin

Top photo:
Cynthia with
daughters Marlena &
Sarah

Bottom photo
Cynthia with
grandsons Domenick
& Trustin

Cynthia's parents
Emma and Nelson
Yates

Chapter 5

PIECES OF THE STORMS

In August of 2004, I had a chance to visit my cousin who lives in Florida. Since Marlena was going on vacation with her siblings, I welcomed the change of scenery. I was in desperate need of relaxation and a vacation to forget about all of my problems and responsibilities. It is always exciting to me, when it comes to flying; I am like a little child. I have taught my grandsons, as the plane takes off to look down upon the tree tops, they look like bunches of broccoli. The clouds are so fluffy and beautiful; they remind me of oversized cotton candy, as they float by, and the tiny houses and cars look like a board game. My grandsons love to fly probably as much as I do.

My vacation was just what the doctor ordered, no stress! My cousin picked me up at the airport, and as we traveled to her home, the excitement overwhelmed me. You could hear the joy in my voice as I said, "No cooking, no cleaning, or yard work and I did not have to take care of any one, but myself." We always had a great time when I went to visit. I could not wait to see the ocean, smell the fresh air, and feel the warmth of the sun on my face. Our conversation was interrupted when her cell phone rang. It was her friend telling us to be careful because the weather was really getting bad. We did drive through some terrible storms, and the first thing we did when we arrived at her home, was turn on the television. The words on the bottom of the screen flashed to let people know they needed to evacuate as quickly as possible. We did not have to worry because the storm was not coming our way. That was the good news; however, with all of the rain, I would not be able to see the ocean any time soon. My vacation went by so quickly, but we did not get to do much because of the bad weather. We made the best of it though and still had fun anyway.

The day before I was to return home, the path of the storm changed, we did not have any time to leave the area, because we were in the path of Hurricane Charley. The wind sounded like a freight train! The only part of her home without any windows was the laundry room. We waited in that area, until the storm subsided and all was calm, before we ventured outside to check out the damage. This was surely not the sunshine state, with the sunny weather I remembered and loved. I did have to reschedule my flight because the airport was hit so badly that part of the roof had been blown away. It was strange to see, inside of the airport, people holding umbrellas over their heads, as big raindrops fell to the floor. I was thankful to finally be boarding the airplane and to know that piece of my life was over.

Luke 24:8 (The disciples went and woke him, saying, "Master, Master, we're going to drown!" He got up and rebuked the wind and the raging waters; the storm subsided, and all was calm.) (NIV)

The next storm, would hit even harder and this piece in my life will never be forgotten. The day of my friend's wedding rehearsal, which should have been a happy occasion for me, since I was one of the bridesmaids, was overshadowed with Mom's diagnosis of cancer. Mom was disappointed to miss such a wonderful occasion, but even with her bad news, she still wanted me to go to support my friend on her special day.

A short time after mom returned home, I again reluctantly, left her for a few days to travel to Texas. I had tickets bought for me as a birthday gift, to watch a Steeler football game. Of course Mom told me to go; she didn't want me to miss out on any opportunity to travel. I had mixed emotions about going, but I did want to attend a service at Lakewood Church. Mom knew that was a dream of mine, to hear Pastor Joel Osteen preach in person. I did decide to make the trip; we saw the game and the Steelers even won. Better yet, I did get to worship at Lakewood Church. It is amazing to see so many members that follow Pastor Osteen's teachings; he is one that really has favor with the Lord. Out of all those people, Pastor Joel prayed for me, "God's favor was truly on my life that day!"

Exodus 33:12 (Moses said to the Lord, "You have been telling me, lead these people, but you have not let me know whom you will send with me. You have said, "I know you by name and you have found favor with me." (NIV)

But I could not wait to get back home to be with my mother. After returning, this would be the start of a long and painful journey. Mom's cancer had spread and she would need a major operation. The doctors involved in her case did not give us any hope; they believed she only had six months to live. If Mom would agree to have the operation, she would have a lot of factors against her; she had a hard time fighting off infections, she had open heart surgery about ten years ago, and her age was the biggest to be considered. Even after the physicians' professional opinions, Mom still decided to have the cancer surgery.

On October 18th was a day that would change Mom's life forever. We both joked around about flagging down a taxi and running away, so she would not have to go through such an ordeal. The nurse came in and explained the procedure very carefully, so Mom knew what to expect when everything was over. As I sat in the waiting area,

with a Bible in my hand, I remembered how many times
Mom had constantly prayed for everyone, and now it was
our turn. Our family filled the waiting room, and we all
had a lot of time to pray, because her operation took about
eight hours. When the time finally came and we had the
chance to go and see her, it was nothing anyone could have
ever prepared me for. It was a frightening sight to see all of
those tubes everywhere.

Unfortunately, Mom contracted a staph infection
and needed six weeks of intravenous medications at home.
I was in for the shock of my life with the care Mom needed.
Over the course of time, she was hospitalized five times
and we were told over and over they thought she would not
live much longer. The emergency department staff knew
us by our first names. She had constant struggles with
health issues that we knew would never end, but she kept
up a good fight. Even with all of her limitations and

challenges, she did what she was able. Nothing stopped her from living life to the fullest and with a sweet spirit. It truly amazed me how much Mom went through and did not complain. I guess knowing you are deathly ill, you appreciate the gift of life and hold onto it with everything you have.

I could not believe how much time and energy went into Mom's care. Mom said that she was blessed to have six children, grandchildren, a wonderful sister, and a great friend, to help her out in her time of need. We all played a big role in Mom's care, but I was at her side daily and when new problems would arise that needed extra attention, I made three or four more trips back and forth a day. I was on call twenty-four hours; I became so tired and burned out, I often thought, "How much longer can I possibly go on like this?" I felt so guilty thinking of myself when she was the one who had to endure all of the pain and suffering. No matter what she went through and how bad her situation became, she continued to pray and put the needs of others before her own. I never heard her say, not even once, that she wanted to give up. All of her doctors called her, "A walking miracle!" They could not believe how she was still here with the cancer so advanced. She lived three years over the time they had given her and was still going. Her will to live was unbelievable, and with God's sufficient grace, she continued to move forward.

2 Corinthians 12:9 (But he said to me, "My grace is sufficient for you, for my power is made perfect in weakness.) (NIV)

After Mom's last time to be hospitalized, she was sent home on March sixth, in the care of hospice, and we knew no matter how hard she fought, her battle would eventually be lost. They gave her only a couple of weeks until this horrible disease would consume her life. Two weeks passed and her faith continued to be stronger than ever, even with all of the pain and suffering. Easter came and it was hard to enjoy our meal, with all of the trimmings, while Mom ate a popsicle in bed, but she would not have it any other way. We knew it was hard for her to tolerate the smell of the different foods, but she insisted that the odors did not make her sick, so everyone would eat.

Mom's relatives and friends came to visit her daily; everyone would enjoy a popsicle as they sat at her bedside. Laughter filled the air as they joked around about the good old times, to enlighten the anticipation of what was to come in the days ahead. One evening, a relative shared with Mom, that her cousin bought a floral and gift shop in Perryopolis. I heard the excitement in Mom's voice that she wanted to see that shop. The next day she told me she would love to take a ride to enjoy the sunshine and a little fresh air. She wasn't fooling me; she had a mission to accomplish, and I knew whatever it took, I would not be the one to stand in her way.

I cut the tag from her dark blue sweater, an anniversary gift from me, which she never had the chance to wear. After I had her dressed, the next step was the stairs; very slowly she did eventually make it to the car. She sat in the back with her sister, propped up on pillows and under a blanket. I often wonder what went on in Mom's mind as she took her last ride. She went on this road so many times, but what did she see through her eyes on this trip? She did give me orders where to drive and who she wanted to see. Amazingly, she stayed awake the whole time, and although she could not get out of the car to go into the flower shop, she was perfectly content when she saw her cousin and the outside of the shop. Mom continued to surprise everyone, and nobody could believe what an accomplishment for somebody so sick to achieve. I was thankful for the Grace of God in Mom's life.

1 Corinthians 15:10 (But by the grace of God I am what I am, and his grace to me was not without effect. No, I worked harder than all of them---yet not I, but the grace of God that was with me.) (NIV)

I could not begin to put into words, the agony and heartache I felt, as I watched my mother struggle to live. We all took our turn, at her bedside, to do whatever we could to make her comfortable. I felt helpless as I looked at her fragile body; it was hard to imagine how healthy she once was. I had flashbacks of the past, how she giggled as she pushed my little brothers around in a wheelbarrow, how she helped my father put their tents up so they could sleep out in the back yard, how she chaperoned my ninth grade dance for school, and how she held my hand so I would not get lost in a massive crowd of people. Now I was sitting at her bedside, reading the Bible to her and holding her hand so she knew she was not alone. With what little strength she had left, she tapped me on my hand with her little finger to reassure me that she was alright. Even in her last hour, she continued to comfort me.

There were a lot of last pieces in Mom's life, her last ride, her last dance, her last puzzle, her last meal, her last word, her last tear, her last smile, and her last breath. And she would not know, but I would help the nurse take care of her, and I would paint her fingernails one last time. On May, 3, 2009, my mother went home to be with the Lord.

2 Corinthians 5:8 (We are confident, I say, and would prefer to be away from the body and at home with the Lord.") (NIV)

After Mom passed away, I experienced so many different emotions at one time. First of all, I was glad because I knew her pain and suffering were finally over. The last piece of her life had been completed. Since Mom was such a big piece of my life, I felt alone, afraid, empty and lost; it felt like all of the pieces to my life had been broken. It was truly hard on me; we had shared so much love and time together, and grown so close. We definitely built a loving friendship and relationship between a mother and her daughter. That is what happens when you spend a lot of time with God. You get close and build a loving friendship and relationship with Him also. As I pick the pieces up, one at a time, I experience God's comfort and peace; I know because of what my mother believed, she

lives on in eternity.

John 3:16 ("For God so loved the world that he gave his
one and only Son, that whoever believes in him shall not
perish but have eternal life.") (NIV)

Dear Reader,

Do you have a loved one who has gone home to be with the Lord?

Are you feeling alone, afraid, or lost?

Remember: The Holy Spirit came to give us comfort and peace!

Chapter 6

A Piece of Heaven

No matter what lies ahead in my future, I know each new day is a gift from God. I have shared many trials, tribulations, blessings and miracles in the pages of this book, and still left out countless pieces to my journey in life. For as long as I could remember, I have told my youngest brother that when we endure hardships and heartache, it builds character and we will grow emotionally and spiritually. During these difficulties, it is our choice to make; will we hold onto the promises in God's word, or give up? In John 8:31-32, Jesus said to the Jews who had believed him, ("If you hold onto my teaching, you are really my disciples. Then you will know the truth, and the truth will set you free.")(NIV) Isn't that what life is all about? All of us want to be free from heartache, and to experience God's presence every day. The Bible teaches that we have been adopted into the family of God. In Ephesians 1:5, states, ("He predestined us to be adopted as His sons through Jesus Christ, in accordance with his pleasure and will.") (NIV) We are heirs with Jesus. As Christians, we have been made beneficiaries of every spiritual blessing that belongs to and comes from the heavenly realm. (NIV) Since I believe that I have been adopted into the family of God, I know God as my Heavenly Father, Jesus as my Heavenly Brother, and the Holy Spirit as my Heavenly Friend. I am not an ordinary person; I am a child of the Most High God, and I live everyday with a piece of heaven on earth.

September 16, 2009

Dear Friend,

I have shared many of the bits and pieces in my journey of life, how God has changed the life of an ordinary person. In chapter one, I shared that everyone needs quiet time and to be alone to pray. In Chapter two, we must give thanks and believe that God does answer prayer. God is the same today as He was yesterday, and He still does miracles. And in chapter three, as we learn to trust in God's unfailing love, we will experience His compassion and love for us. In chapter four, God is always with us, and we have to make the choice to go to Him with faith and confidence, so that we may receive mercy and grace to help us in our time of need. In my journey, there have been many trials and tribulations with plenty of tears, but remember chapter five, the Holy Spirit came to give us comfort and peace. Finally, chapter six reminds us to hold onto the promises in God's word, because each new day is a precious gift from God! My prayer for you, dear friend, is that you would know God as your Heavenly Father, and live everyday with a piece of Heaven on earth.

God's blessing is wished to all,

Cynthia Yates Soles

ACKNOWLEDGMENTS

I would like to extend my appreciation and sincere gratitude to so many special family members and friends who have helped me, in my life's journey, and in writing this book!

First, I would like to thank God for blessing me with such a special father, Nelson Yates. Watching him devote his life to caring, giving, and loving many, is a true testimony for a gracious caregiver. His wonderful example has taught me important values, and he has been an inspiration to me.

I would like to extend my heartfelt gratitude to my siblings, Freda, Nelson Jr., John, Mark, Wayne, and to their families. All of their love, help, and support, over the past years, has blessed my life.

I also heartily acknowledge Brian Campbell, whose help, encouragement, and support in this process has been deeply appreciated. His giving to so many people without expecting anything in return has been an inspiration on my life.

I wish to extend sincere thanks to Chuck Muia and Karen Kassa, at Muia Studio, of Donora, Pennsylvania, for the photos on the jacket of this book. Their time, talent, and friendship are deeply appreciated.

I would like to thank Dorothy Fox, from the bottom of my heart, because she has always gone out of her way to listen, encourage, pray, and share her wisdom about God. Her life shows a true reflection of Christ's love.

Special thanks to: Sylvia, Rose Ellen, Barbara, Cathy, Sherry, Joy, Ranel, Beverly, Judy, Arlene, Norma, Karen, Mike, Bob, Denise, Jeanne, Vicki, Debbie, Diane, Cindee, Concetta, Adrienne, Natalina, Donna, Deana, Sue, Aunt Martha and her family, my aunts, uncles, cousins, friends on the internet (especially Mark), and the faithful Christians of Salvation House, just to name a few! I could go on and on, with so many others who have shared their lives with me. Their support, encouragement, faith, prayers, and love have blessed me dearly.

I appreciate the time and knowledge which Barbara Vandermer has donated to the editing of this book. Her sincere dedication to teach and minister has inspired not only me, but many others as well. Her faith and support she shared with me for more than thirty years has touched my heart, and it has been a great learning experience to work by her side.

Finally, I would like to thank Carol Otto for donating so much of her time, support, encouragement, and computer skills she brought to this project. Her love and faithful prayers for so many have made a great impression on my life. I am grateful for her wonderful friendship, loyalty, and expertise in making this book a reality.

CPSIA information can be obtained at www.ICGtesting.com
Printed in the USA
BVOW032012041212

307307BV00002B/22/P